# WOW! Explained

## Welcome...

to another great edition of *WOW!* In this issue we will be looking at lots of things that need explaining! Find out what an astronomer does, how to become an astronaut, and if teleportation is really possible. We've got loads more awesome stuff for you to read, too. Plus we're lucky enough to be able to welcome back four special guest editors – Max, Cat, Ant and Tiger.

Penny Piminy

Editor in Chief

## What's inside...

# The Collector theory

What are you DOING?
Just p … p … playing.
It is a Saturday.

There is no time for *playing!*
My cars!

There's a call for you, sir. It's the office.
Thank you, Jones. I'm just coming. Get back to work, Archibald.

When I grow up I'm going to get everything I want.

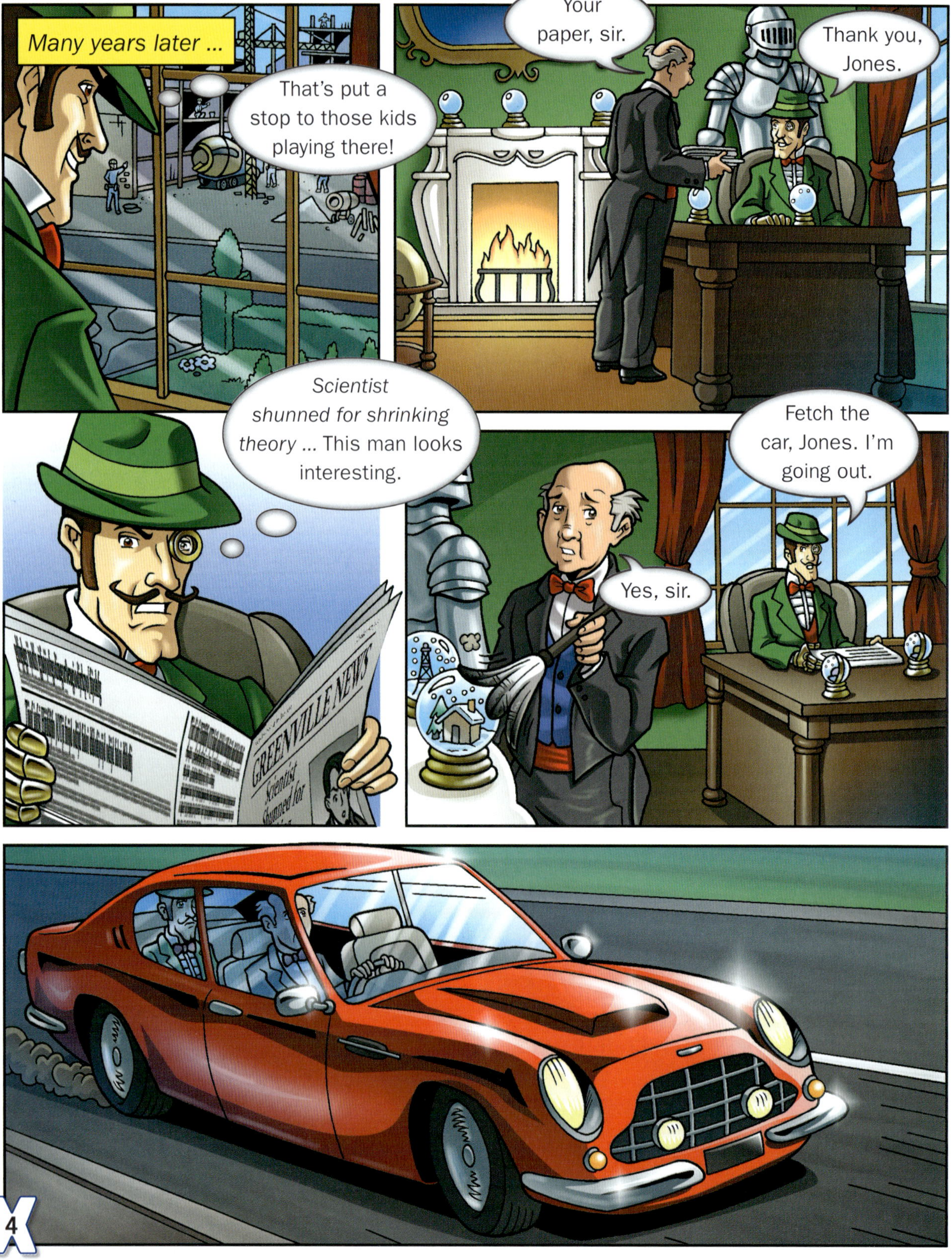

*Many years later ...*

That's put a stop to those kids playing there!

Your paper, sir.

Thank you, Jones.

*Scientist shunned for shrinking theory* ... This man looks interesting.

GREENVILLE NEWS

Fetch the car, Jones. I'm going out.

Yes, sir.

**This is just one theory about why the Collector is like he is. Can you think of any others? You could make up a story about how he got his bionic arm.**

# Making money …

So, how is money made in the first place?

*If there's not enough money in the world, why can't we just make more?* It seems a simple solution, doesn't it? If we make more money and give everyone lots, then people would be richer, right? Wrong. Unfortunately, it doesn't work like that.

Think of it as a sticker collection (or anything else that you might have collected). The most special ones, the most collectable ones, are the ones that you can't get many of. They are worth more because there are less of them around. If you could suddenly get hold of lots of the most valuable stickers, then they would not be so collectable. It's the same with money.

Each coin or note printed has a value attached to it. But if there is suddenly a lot more money printed, then the value of each coin or note goes down. Each one would not be so special. The effect of printing more money is that it would raise prices of everything so you would need even more money to pay for the things you needed!

## Coins

There are three stages involved with making coins: making blanks, making dies, and striking the coins.

**Blanks** (blank discs that form the basis of the coin)

Coins are made of mixtures of different metals called alloys. The alloys are melted in a furnace. A long strip of metal comes out, which is cut and rolled to make it thinner.

The metal is then made into blank metal discs. These are punched by a machine called a *press*. At the Royal Mint in the UK, about 10 000 discs are produced in a minute.

This photo shows coins being made at La Monnaie de Paris (The Paris Mint).

**Dies** (parts of a machine that strike the pattern on to the blanks)

Each type of coin has a different design on it. Once the design has been created, a plaster model of it is made. This is scanned into a computer. The computer then guides an engraving machine on to a piece of steel. This piece is called the *reduction punch*. It is used to make the dies.

An engraving machine cuts a design on to a reduction punch.

**Striking coins** (the process of printing the pattern on to blanks)

Blanks go in to a coining press that has two dies (one on each side). Pressure of about 60 tonnes is applied as the dies hit the blanks.

# Notes

As with coins, designers create designs which are engraved on to metal. These form the dies. The dies are then put under pressure and heated so that an impression of the design is transferred on to a metal printing plate. The plates are covered in ink for the printing process.

The sheets are checked carefully – they have to be perfect. They then go for overprinting. This is when the national seals and serial numbers are added. Then a machine cuts the sheets into individual notes.

Here, sheets of Euro banknotes are being cut into individual notes.

**Did you know ...**

- Designs are first created by hand – not using computers. This makes them harder to copy.
- 'Paper' money is made of cotton mixed with linen to make it durable. Before World War I, it was made of silk.
- In the USA, the design of notes alters every 7 to 10 years.
- Paper money originated in the 8th century in China.
- Banknotes have been issued by the Bank of England for over 300 years.

# The Master-bot revealed

The Master-bot is a robot used by a villain known as the Collector. It is much larger than previous X-bots. The Master-bot can think and talk for itself and is extremely aggressive. If spotted, it should not be approached.

The Collector is a master criminal with one goal – to own the biggest collection of snow globes in the world. He likes to cause mischief and mayhem (see pages 2–5 and 38–39 for more about the Collector).

**Spikes:** the Master-bot uses these to defend itself if anything tries to attack it from above.

**Shrink mode:** this allows the Master-bot to shrink and steal valuable objects. The dial turns anticlockwise until the arrowheads around the watch line up to form Xs. A large, red X appears on the watch face. This can then be pointed at the object it wants to shrink.

**Limited speech:** unlike other X-bots, the Master-bot can talk. It has been known to say things like "Must collect", "You are in my way", and "Destroy". It clearly has anger issues.

**Multifunctional storage:** the back and belly of the Master-bot can open up. Here, it keeps its rotor blades used for flying, its shark-like fin used for swimming, and its claw that it uses for gripping and collecting things. In can also store glass globes and smaller X-bots.

**Feet:** these are used when walking, taking off and landing. They also store flotation devices which allow the Master-bot to float on water.

# X-bot upgrades

## X5

**Primary aim:** Protecting the Master-bot

**Uses:** Attacking, Defending, Tracking, Flying, Floating, Swimming, Digging

**Tools:** Eye cameras, Sharp jaws, Helicopter blades, Foot floats, Nosed drill, Glue cannon, Cutting tool, Fins, Propeller

**Other:** Can work together in pairs or shoals (when swimming)

**Strengths:** Very aggressive

**Weaknesses:** Crashing, Hungry seals

**NASTI rating:** X X X X X

## X-bot Bee

**Primary aim:** Collecting real bees from around the world

**Uses:** Defending hive, Flying, Attacking

**Tools:** Eye cameras, Bee camouflage, Sharp jaws, Electro-charged stinger, Helicopter blades

**Strengths:** Good at dancing, Looks like a bee

**Weaknesses:** Crashing

**NASTI rating:** X X X X X

**Things to do**

Invent your own X-bot. What can it do? What functions does it have?

# Bees and the end of the world

The Collector once used his X-bots to try to steal all the bees in the world. What would have happened if he had succeeded?

## Pollination

Pollen looks like a powder or dust. In order for flowers to produce seeds (and therefore produce new flowers), pollen needs to move from one flower to another. This is called pollination.

Greenville's most up-to-date news

Saturday 1[illegible]arch

# GREENVILLE NEWS

## What Can The Matter Bee?

Today the science world is buzzing with speculation. Swarms of bees all over the world are disappearing and nobody seems to know why. The disappearance of bee colonies may not just mean the end of honey production everywhere, but the very end of life itself!

The famous physicist, Albert Einstein, warned that if bees disappeared from the planet then humans would be extinct within four years! When bees fly from plant to plant to collect nectar, they spread pollen. This fertilizes plants. No bees means no more plants, no more food and no more us!

### Did you know ...

- 90% of all flowers are pollinated with the help of living creatures. The other 10% are pollinated by wind and water.
- Creatures who carry pollen are called pollinators.
- There are approx 200 000 kinds of pollinators.
- Most pollinators are insects (bees, wasps, moths, butterflies, etc) but there are other pollinators too (birds and bats).

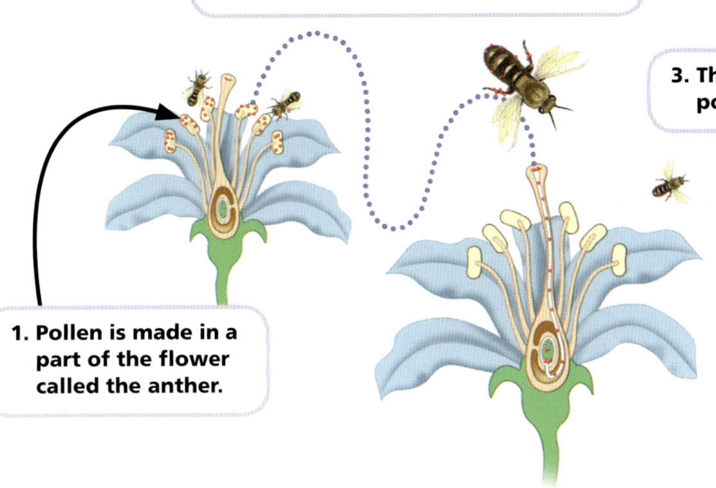


## Bees as pollinators

Bees feed on a sticky substance called nectar. Nectar is sweet and gives bees lots of energy. It is produced by flowers to attract bees. While the bees are feeding on nectar, pollen grains stick to their hind legs. When they fly to the next flower, they brush the pollen off. This pollen is then used by the new flower to fertilize their eggs and make the seeds.

Pollen grains stick to the hairs on the bee's legs.

Bees are vital to our ecosystems. About $\frac{1}{5}$ of all global food production and possibly $\frac{2}{3}$ of all major crops depend on pollination by animals – mainly bees. If bees disappeared then crops would fail. All the animals that depend on the crops would not be able to survive – the effect would be catastrophic. We depend on plants and animals to live. This is why the scientist Albert Einstein said that if there were no more bees left in the world then the human race would not be able to survive. (For more on Albert Einstein see page 20.)

**Bee facts ...**

- Bees are found on every continent except Antarctica.
- There are around 20 000 different species of bee.
- Bees have long tongues so they can reach the nectar.
- Apiculture is another name for bee-keeping.
- Being fuzzy is useful – electrostatic charge helps pollen stick to them!

# THE GREAT GIZA MYSTERY

There are still many mysteries in the world, but none more baffling than the Great Pyramid at Giza, in Egypt. Every year, hundreds of tourists flock to see it. But how was it built, and why?

**What are pyramids?**
Most pyramids are burial chambers for the Pharaohs of ancient Egypt. There are over 100 pyramids in Egypt. The Great Pyramid is the biggest.

**How many people built it?**
Most archaeologists agree that the Great Pyramid was built by up to 25 000 people. These included: quarry workers, masons, ramp builders, toolmakers, and food, clothing and fuel suppliers.

**How big is it?**
It was originally about 146 metres high, but it has lost about 10 metres over the years because of erosion. Its base length is 230 metres. The total mass is estimated at 5.9 million tonnes.

**Who was the Great Pyramid built for?**
It is thought that it was built for the Egyptian king, Khufu.

**How long did it take to build?**
About 20 years or more. It was built in around 2560 BC.

**How was it built?**
This question has puzzled historians and archaeologists for years. With no modern machinery it was an awesome task. Here is what most archaeologists think …

- It is not known exactly what tools were used to get the stones out of the rocks where they were quarried, but each block weighs more than a ton!
- A system of ramps was used to drag the millions of blocks into position.
- They probably lifted the blocks using wooden and bronze levers.
- The pyramid was built by aligning it closely to certain star constellations.

**Did you know …**

We still use Egyptian design in our buildings today. Another famous pyramid in Paris forms part of the entrance to the Louvre museum.

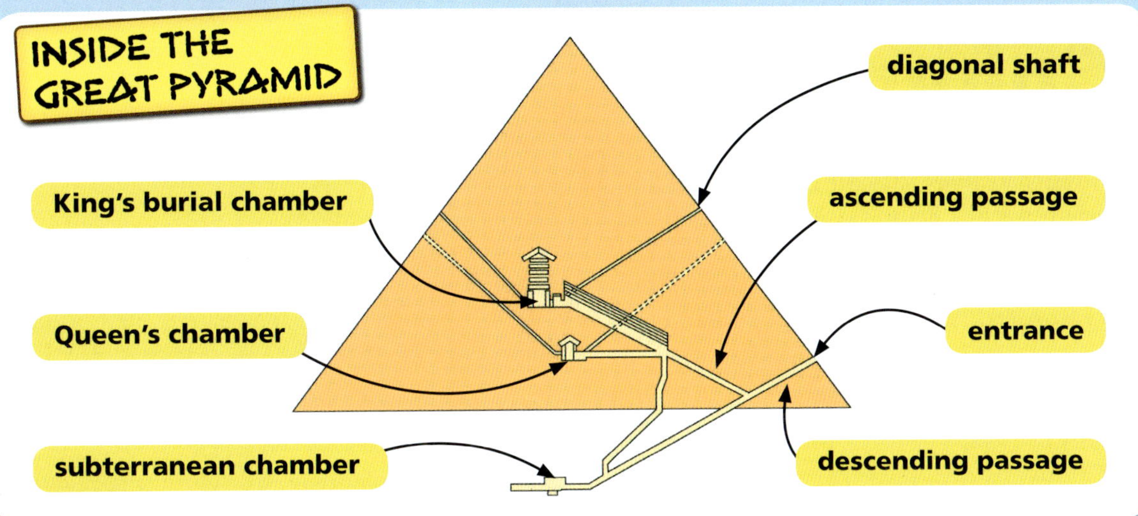


## The Sphinx

The Sphinx is another mystery at Giza. It is a massive stone statue with the body of a lion and the head of a human. No one is certain when the Sphinx was built, but it is thought to be over 4500 years old!

The nose on the face of the Sphinx is missing. It is thought that this was broken off by a cannon ball fired by soldiers of Napoleon (Napoleon was a French general and ruler, 1769–1821).

Did you know that the ancient Egyptians used to worship cats?

### Did you know ...

It was the Egyptians that first kept cats as pets – over 4000 years ago! When a domestic cat died, their owners would go into mourning and shave their eyebrows as a sign of grief. Cats were protected by Egyptian law. If a human killed a cat (whether it was on purpose or not) then they were sentenced to death.

# Sphereing

Have you ever kicked or thrown a ball down a hill? Imagine what it would be like to be inside it!

Sphereing (also known as *Zorbing*) is a crazy, adrenalin-fuelled sport. A person is put in a large transparent (see-through) ball and rolled down a hill!

The balls are made of plastic. There is an inner sphere and an outer sphere. A layer of air is trapped between the spheres to absorb shock. This way, the person, or people, in the inner sphere is/are protected.

The longest sphereing ride is recorded in the Guinness Book of World Records as being 570 metres. The fastest ride was recorded as 52 kilometres per hour (32 miles per hour).

These people are secured in, waiting to go!

**Did you know ...**

The Guinness Book of World Records (formerly the Guinness Book of Records) was first published in 1954. It is a reference book that details record-breaking achievements by people and those found in nature.

**Warning, kids!**

Don't try this at home unless you have the proper equipment and the proper training and supervision.

# WOW!
## Space Special

# Star gazing

Have you ever looked up at the night sky and wondered what is really up there? Scientists are constantly looking for new ways to unlock the secrets of the universe. They use large telescopes to magnify distant objects so that they can study them.

**How do telescopes work?**

The main telescopes used are called optical telescopes. They work by using curved lenses or mirrors to gather light. There are three different types of optical telescope:

- refracting telescopes which use glass lenses
- reflecting telescopes which use mirrors
- catadioptric telescopes which use lenses and mirrors.

Gemini North Observatory on Mauna Kea, Hawaii.

**Refracting**

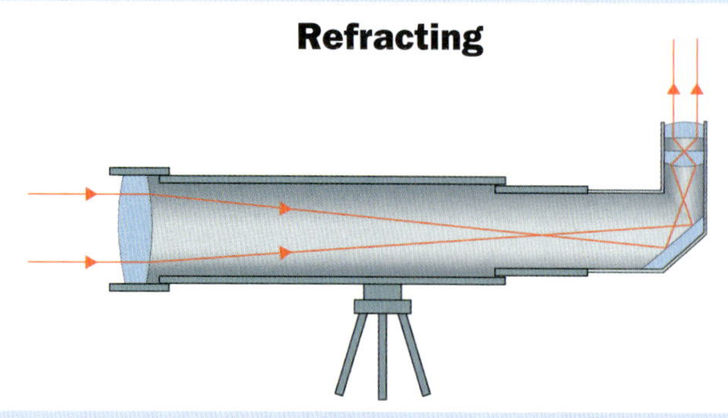

A large lens gathers the light. It bends or *refracts* the light to a point near the back of the tube. A small eyepiece lens brings the image to your eye and magnifies the image.

**Reflecting**

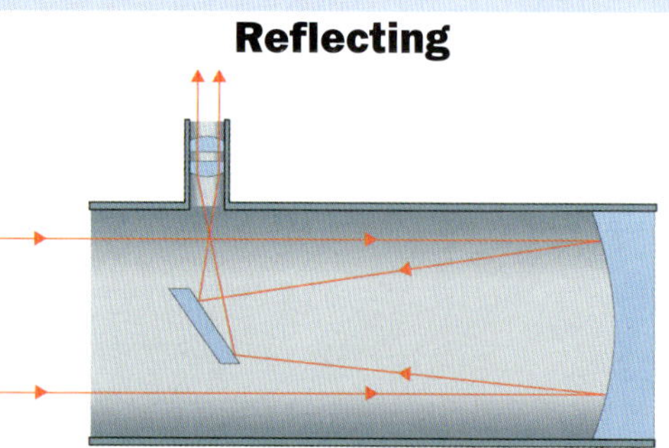

Light is bounced off mirrors, rather than bent by lenses, through to the eyepiece.

The larger the size of lens or mirror, the more light the telescope collects and the brighter the final image.

# Some of the world's largest optical telescopes

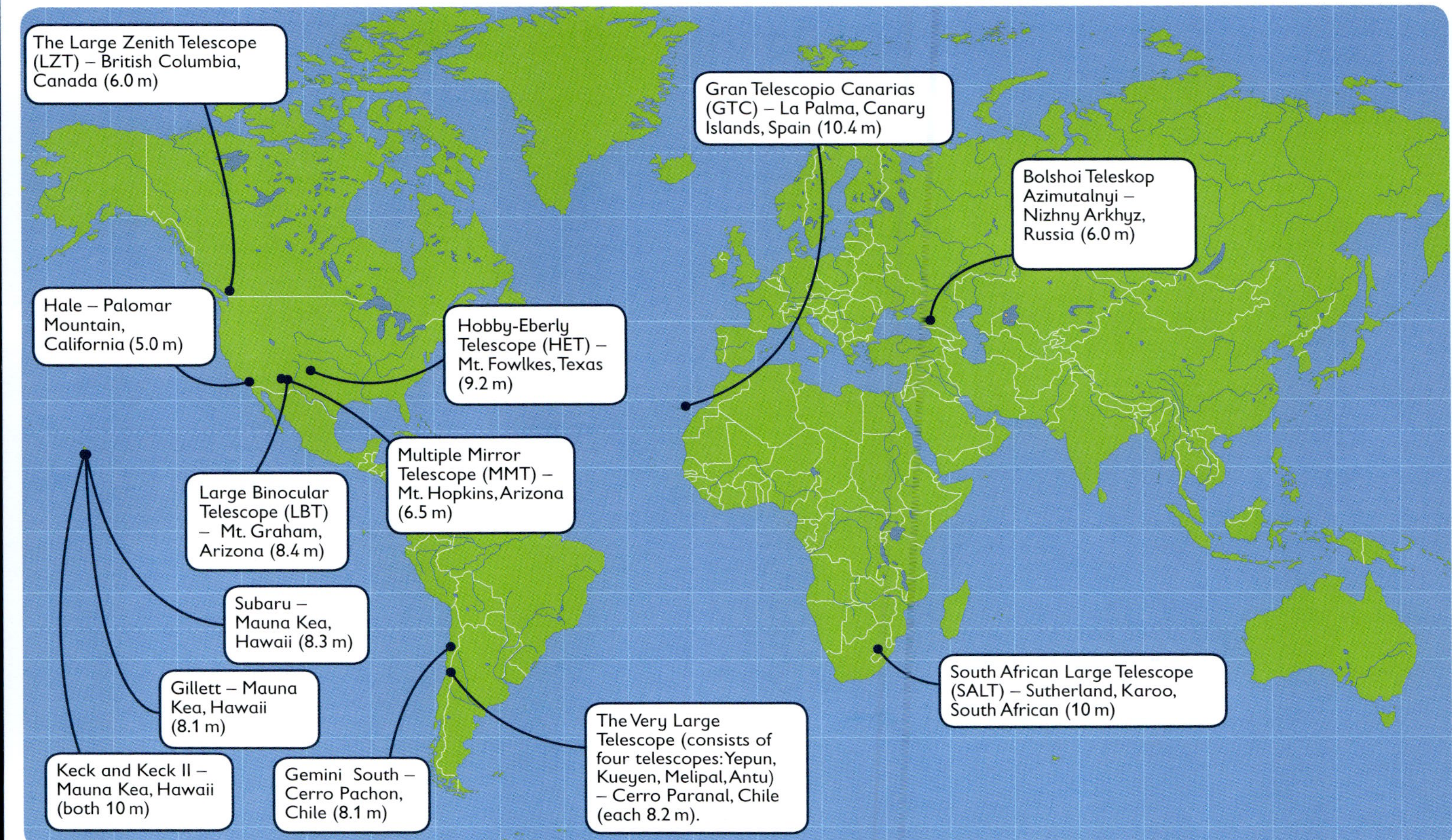


All the measurements stand for the diameter of the lens in metres.

# Through the lens ...

What can scientists see when they look into space? Do you know the difference between a planet and a star? And what is dark matter? Here are a few of the answers ...

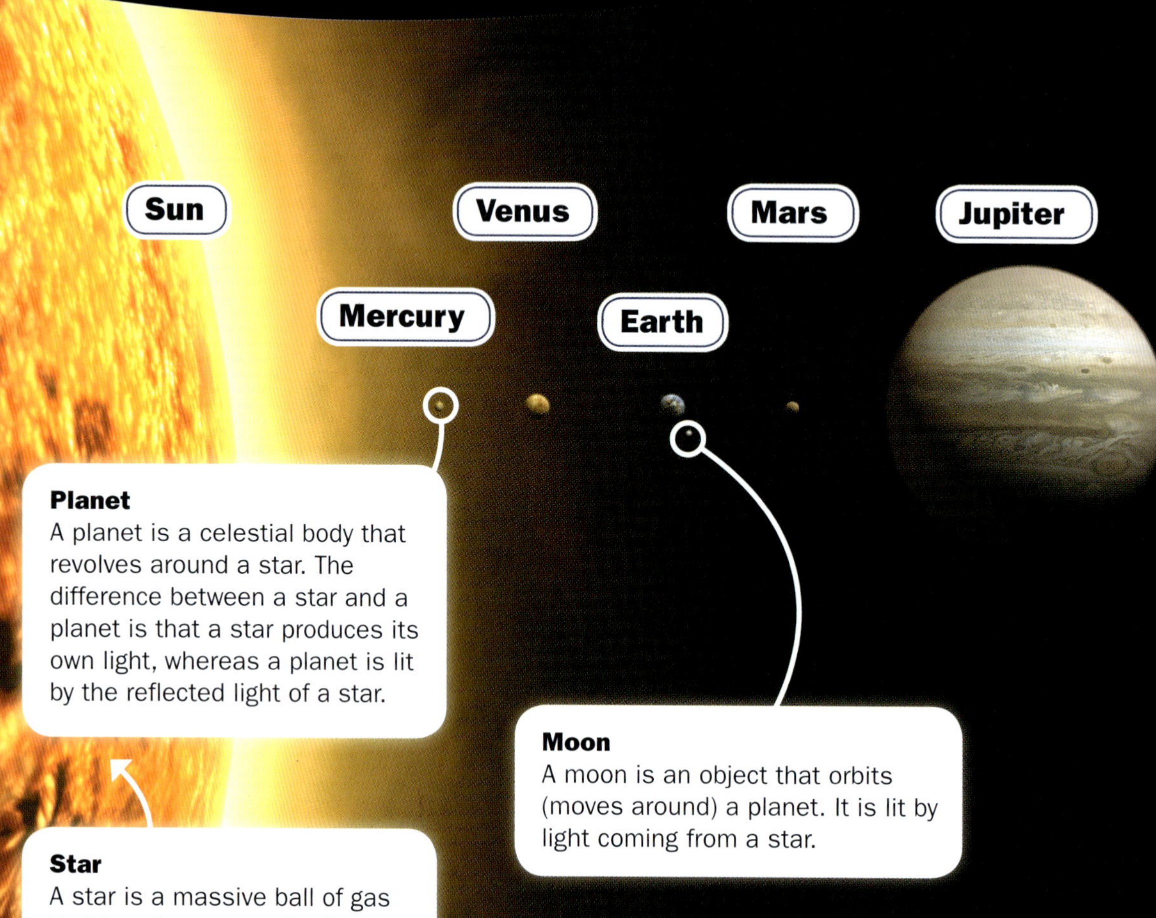


**Planet**
A planet is a celestial body that revolves around a star. The difference between a star and a planet is that a star produces its own light, whereas a planet is lit by the reflected light of a star.

**Moon**
A moon is an object that orbits (moves around) a planet. It is lit by light coming from a star.

**Star**
A star is a massive ball of gas that has its own gravity. A star emits (gives off) light and heat. Stars vary in how bright or hot they are. The Sun is a star. It is the nearest star to Earth.

**Dark matter**
Dark matter is thought to be the matter that makes up most of the universe. The only problem is ... you can't see it! You can't see it because it doesn't glow. So no one is quite sure what it is. However, they know it is there because of the way it works with gravity and because of how stars and galaxies move and rotate.

**Comet**
A comet is a body of ice, dust, and gas that orbits the Sun. When it gets near to the Sun, the heat from the Sun turns the outer ice into gas and the solid particles are released as dust. This forms a bright tail. The tail can be several hundred million kilometres long.

**Saturn**

**Uranus**

**Neptune**

**Meteoroid**
A meteoroid is a piece of comet debris that orbits the Sun. It is a small body of stony or metallic fragments. Most meteroids are as small as a pebble.

**Pluto**

**Meteorite**
A meteorite is a meteoroid that breaks through the Earth's atmosphere, does not burn up completely, and hits the Earth's surface.

**Supernova**
A supernova is the final explosion of a massive star. It blasts out in a bright, expanding, radioactive wave which gradually fades.

# Time travel ... fact or fiction?

If you could travel in time, when and where would you go? It is a question that has fascinated writers and scientists for many years. But can it actually be done?

The famous scientist Albert Einstein came up with the *Theory of Relativity*. This showed that time is something that can be moved and bent. If time can be bent then, theoretically, it can be bent backwards or forwards, allowing two different points in space and time to meet (for more on Albert Einstein see pages 10–11).

Albert Einstein

**The bend**

Space and time are 'folded' so that there is a shortcut created between two points.

**Black hole**

A black hole is an area of space where the gravity is so strong that no objects can escape being sucked into it. Even light cannot escape – hence the name. They are formed when a star collapses in on itself. But, if a black hole is rotating, then the theory is that a ring is created and that you could go through this hole in the ring – maybe into another place and time.

**Wormhole**

A wormhole is a tunnel between two points in space and time. Two black holes in different places and times are connected. From the outside it would appear that the object would be travelling faster than the speed of light, but in the wormhole the object would be travelling normally.

## The paradox problem

Even if someone could invent a machine to travel in time, there is another major problem. It is called *paradox*. If you go back in time, you could change something that has already happened. You could alter history. It is sometimes known as the 'grandfather paradox'. If you went back in time and somehow prevented your grandfather and grandmother meeting by accident – then you wouldn't have been born – so how could you then go back in time in the first place?

### For

Scientists can't agree whether time travel is possible or not. Professor Amos Ori (from the Technion-Israel Institute of Technology) does believe that time travel could happen and has even designed his own time machine. He argues that if you warp and bend time enough – you create a loop (like a doughnut) and you can travel along the loop. The only problem is no one has figured out how to bend time yet!

### Against

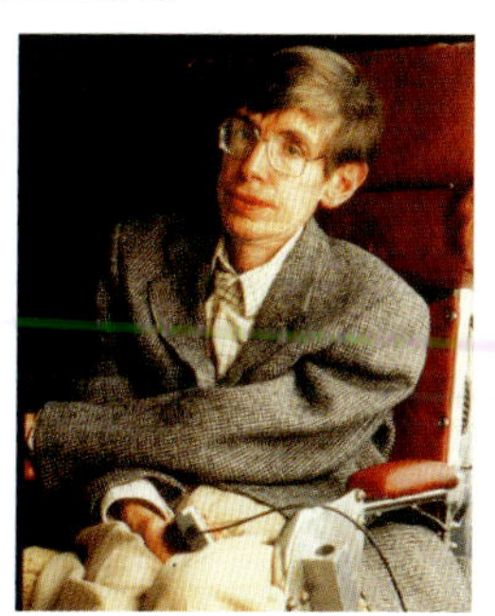

However, others such as the famous physicist, Stephen Hawking, think that if time travel were possible – then we would bump into time-travelling tourists from the future. But we haven't ... he thinks it is highly unlikely.

But the truth is that nobody knows for certain whether time travel is possible ... What do you think?

## Wanted: Time Travellers

In May 2005, students at the Massachusetts Institute of Technology (MIT), USA, organized what they called the first Time Traveller Convention. They invited any time travellers from the future to visit them on a particular date, to prove that time travel was possible. Apparently no one came. Maybe the bus was late.

## Looking back in time

Did you know that you can already *see* back in time? You do it every time you look up at the stars! There is a difference in time between things happening in space and the time it takes for you to see them. For example, the light we see left the Sun about 8 minutes ago ... that's how long it takes light to get from the Sun to Earth. If we look at other stars at night, we are seeing them as they looked like in the past. The fainter the object, the further back in time we are looking.

One of the most famous telescopes is the Hubble Space Telescope. It's in orbit 600 kilometres above Earth. It can see faraway objects more clearly than any other telescope.

Hubble Space Telescope

Sci-fi writers like the idea of time travel. It means that their characters can travel great distances quickly. Can you think of any time travelling characters?

**Why not try writing a story about a time traveller?**

# Day in the life of an astronomer

## By Professor Jim Emerson

*Professor of Astrophysics and Director of Astronomy Unit (Queen Mary, University of London)*

When I get to the University office where I work, the first thing I do is look through the discoveries and ideas that have been posted on the Internet the previous day – to see which are related to my research.

Then I might work on results taken during previous visits to the telescope. I have to turn the images that have been taken into information on all the stars and galaxies that they showed. Each image is taken using coloured filters. Comparing the brightness in the various colours helps me classify the nature, age and distance of objects in the images. I might need to run computer simulations to make predictions about what should be seen. When I am finished, I will post my results on the Internet.

For a few thrilling days a year, I go to the telescope which is in the high, dry Atacama Desert in Chile. I only have a few nights to collect the data I need to test my theories. Everything must be prepared carefully so that no time is wasted. By the time I've finished, I am worn out but happy!

As I fly back to Europe on the aeroplane, I dream about what the new observations might reveal. As I drop off to sleep, I hope that lurking in the data may be something totally unexpected and new. It is enormously exciting to be involved in exploring how our universe, galaxies, stars and planets formed, changed with time, and will change in the future.

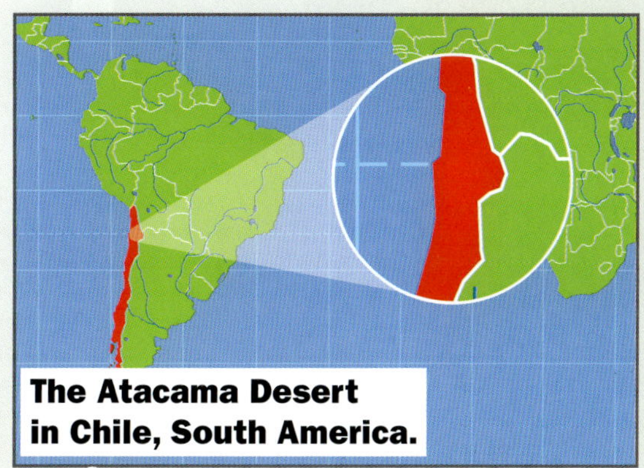

**The Atacama Desert in Chile, South America.**

**Write a blog entry as if you were an astronomer and had just made a new discovery.**

# Living and working in space

Have you ever dreamed of going into space? What do you think it's actually like working up there? Only a lucky few ever get to find out ...

Space shuttle

Space *shuttles* are designed for short flights in space e.g. up to $2\frac{1}{2}$ weeks. They are used to carry out experiments (e.g. trying to grow plants in space), to launch satellites and to carry out repairs.

Space *stations* are permanently in space. Astronauts on board carry out continuous research such as medical research on the effects of living/working in space. They will also carry out maintenance work on the space station.

Space station

**Space sleep**
Imagine going to sleep whilst floating! Astronauts can do this because there is no gravity in space – they are weightless. But for safety (so they don't bump into things) they harness themselves to something fixed such as a wall, seat, or bunk bed inside a cabin.

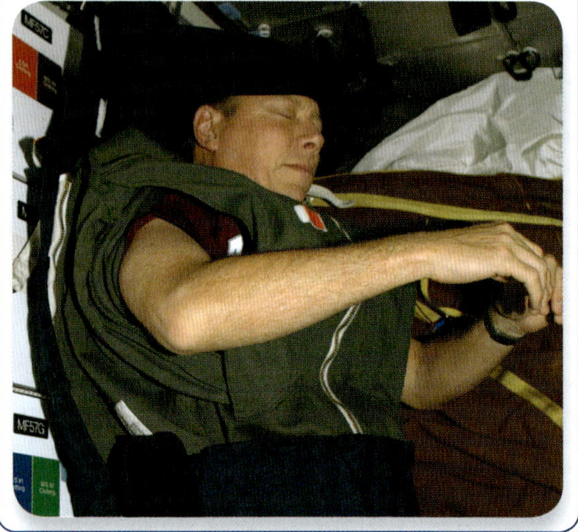

**Hungry?**
Like on Earth, astronauts eat three meals a day. These are carefully planned in order to keep them fit and healthy. Spacecraft have ovens on board but no fridges. All food comes in packets for easy storage. Salt and pepper comes as liquid – if they were in their natural form, they would float away from the food you were trying to sprinkle!

## Nothing to wear?

Astronauts can't wash their clothes – it would be a waste of water. They discard used clothing with other rubbish which is put into a supply vehicle that will burn up in the Earth's atmosphere.

**Inside a space station or space shuttle:** they will generally wear clothes that are comfy and easy to move in, such as shirts, T-shirts, shorts and trousers.

**For take off and landing:** they have special space suits. These are designed to keep the air pressure constant around the astronaut in case of a pressure leak during take off and landing. Also, if the craft lands in cold water (e.g. in the sea) – the suit will keep them warm.

**Working outside:** they use Extra Vehicular Activity (EVA) suits. They can be used for 25 space walks then they have to be returned to Earth to be refurbished. Suits are white because this reflects heat – so astronauts don't get too hot. And white is very visible against the blackness of space. But space walks can also get very cold so the gloves have heaters in them. Suits also include a radio for communication.

**Every drop counts ...**

Yes, astronauts do have baths! But water is very precious in space. They start with a store of water, but then the rest has to be recycled. It is distilled from various sources ... including astronauts' breath! People produce water when they sweat and every time they breathe out. This goes into the air. This air can be condensed in a space craft and made into a water supply!

# Want To Be An Astronaut?

Competition for each job is tough. The training is even tougher ...

**Job available: Pilot**
As a pilot you will control and operate a shuttle. You will be responsible for: safety of the vehicle and its crew, sending out satellites and the success of the mission. You must be highly experienced in flying a range of aircraft including jet aircraft. You must have at least 1000 hours of flying time.

**Job available: Mission specialist**
You will be responsible for operations on board the space shuttle or space station. This will include system control, experiments, space walks and crew planning. You will need a good degree in science or engineering before you can apply.

**Requirements (both positions)**

| | |
|---|---|
| **Fitness:** | must be very fit |
| **Eyesight:** | must be excellent |
| **Blood pressure:** | good (not too high or too low) |
| **Height (Pilot):** | 1.6 m–1.9 m |
| **Height (Mission Specialist):** | 1.48 m–1.9 m |
| **Education:** | degree level (or higher) in science, engineering or maths |

**Training**

1. 1 year basic training – in space technology, science, medical skills, and space station operations, plus scuba diving.
2. 1 year of advanced training – detailed study of space stations, experiments, space vehicles and communication with Mission Control.
3. Following the initial training, you will be given a mission and will be trained with fellow crew members. You will learn specific skills for your mission, experience weightlessness and do virtual reality training. This could take years of preparation.

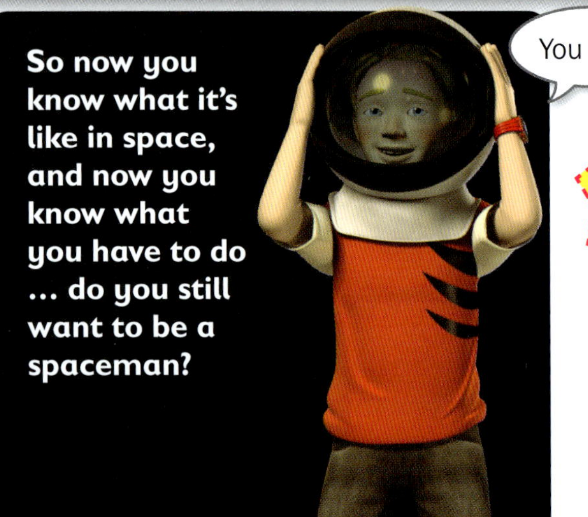


**Things to do**

**Imagine you are already an astronaut. Write a journal of your day . . . you may want to go on a space walk!**

**End of Space Special**

**HIGHLY CONFIDENTIAL**

To: Danni, Day
From: Charles I Sting

Subject: The Collector's fingerprints

Dani,

Today, I had a call from Inspector Textor. He informed me that he has received a snow globe. Inside it was a message. It sounds like the Collector is up to mischief again.

I know that you have had some forensics training. I would like you to run some experiments on this snow globe to see if you can find out anything new. Try and see if you can find any fingerprints. We need this kind of physical evidence if we are going to be able to successfully prosecute him when he is finally caught.

I will have the inspector send the snow globe to you immediately.

Regards,

Charles I. Sting
Director of Operations,
NICE

Turn to page 40 to find out what the message in the snow globe says. Turn over to find out more about forensics!

## FACT FILE: CHARLES I STING

**Likes:** working, reading, and walking his dog, Duke
**Dislikes:** chaos and disorder
**Favourite books:** travel writing, climbing magazines
**Hobbies:** ice climbing, hiking
**Music tastes:** classical
**Favourite food:** curry

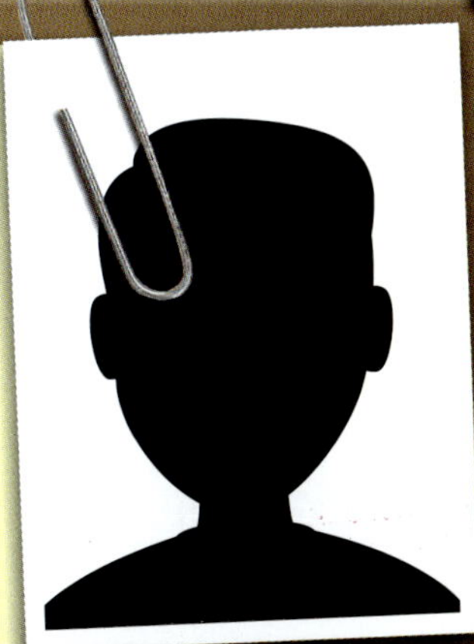

# Crime busters!

Police often rely on scientists to help them solve crimes. But what do they actually do?

**Job profile: Forensic scientist**
Forensic scientists examine material from crime scenes. They provide evidence that can help prove that someone is innocent or guilty of a crime. Their job involves:
- analysing samples (hair, body fluids, glass, paint and drugs)
- attending and examining crime scenes or accidents
- recording findings and collecting evidence
- writing detailed reports and giving evidence in court
- researching and developing new techniques
- meeting with police and offering expert advice.

## Fingerprints

Everyone has a unique fingerprint – a pattern of ridges and bumps on your skin. Your fingerprints stay the same for your whole life. If the skin is damaged it will grow back the same. Even identical twins have different fingerprints.

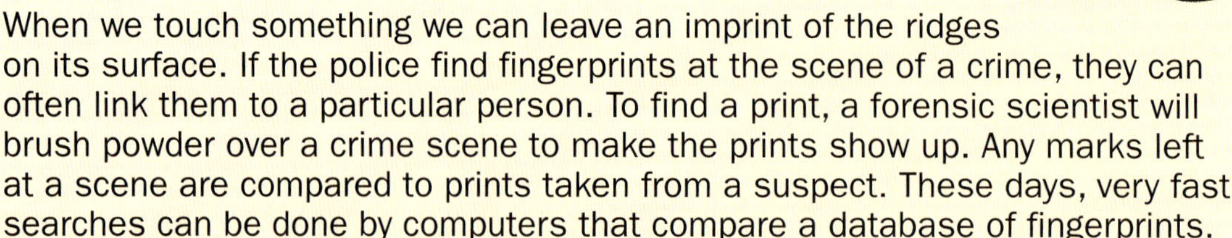

When we touch something we can leave an imprint of the ridges on its surface. If the police find fingerprints at the scene of a crime, they can often link them to a particular person. To find a print, a forensic scientist will brush powder over a crime scene to make the prints show up. Any marks left at a scene are compared to prints taken from a suspect. These days, very fast searches can be done by computers that compare a database of fingerprints.

Fingerprints can fall into 3 general patterns: arch, loop and whorls.

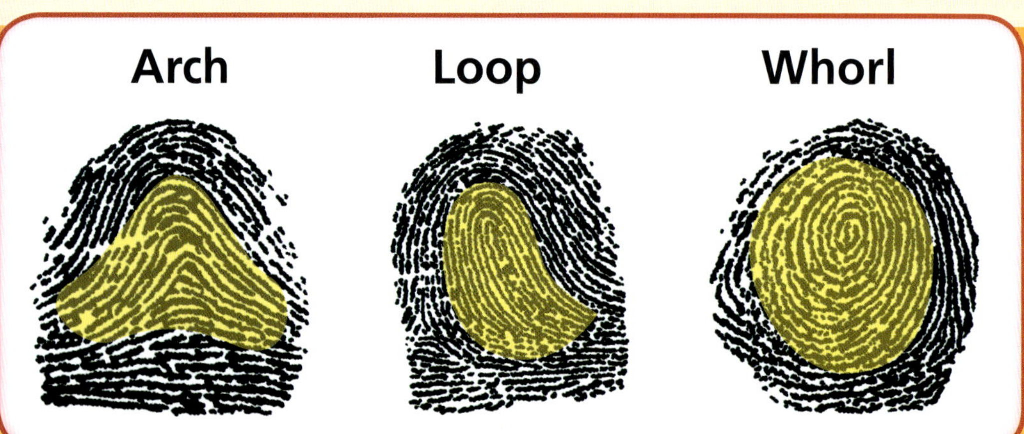

### DNA profiling

DNA profiling is the process of comparing genetic information (found in our hair, blood, sweat and skin) to link a person to a crime scene. DNA profiling is also known as *genetic fingerprinting* because it is similar to traditional fingerprint evidence (they give a unique print of someone). Forensic scientists compare DNA samples taken from the crime scene with a suspect's sample. If they find a match it can prove that the suspect was at the scene of a crime.

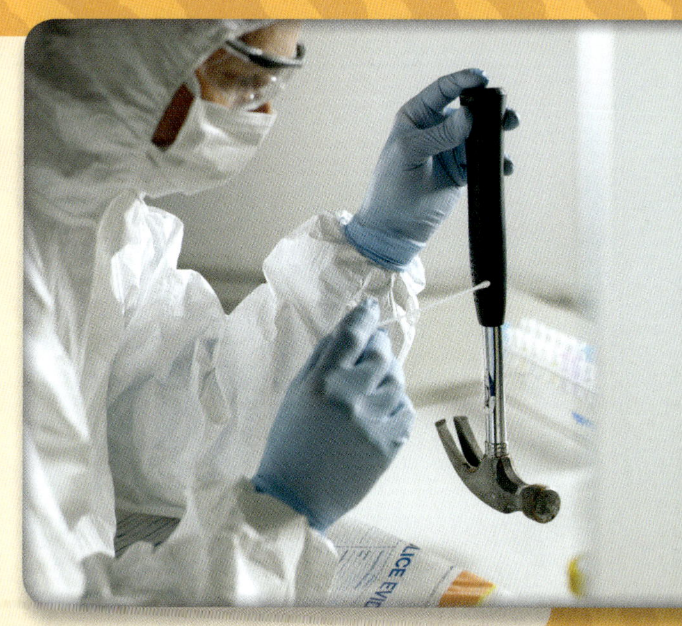

## What is DNA?

DNA is the genetic material found in the cells of all living things. It stores information about what we look like and how we function … it's like a set of instructions. For example, it determines our height, eye colour and hair colour. DNA is unique to every person (except identical twins).

- DNA was first described in 1953 by James Watson and Francis Crick. The scientist Rosalind Franklin also played a big part in deciphering the structure of DNA.
- DNA was first used by police in 1986 in Leicestershire, UK. It helped to clear an innocent suspect – and helped convict someone for murder.
- Early techniques required a lot of high-quality DNA samples to be found at a crime scene. Now, tiny fragments of incomplete DNA can be used.

**Things to do**

**Find a crime story, or a story about a detective. Read the story and write a book review about it.**

**HIGHLY CONFIDENTIAL**

To: Dani, Day
From: Charles I Sting

Subject: RE: The Collector's fingerprints

Latest Wanted poster for the Collector

Dear Charles,

I have run some tests on the snow globe that Inspector Textor sent me. I checked for fingerprints, as you asked. Unfortunately I couldn't find any. The Collector has a bionic hand. I strongly suspect that he only handles the snow globes with this, so that it will not leave any prints. He is a clever villain!

However, I did find a tiny hair on the globe. It must have fallen from his head and stuck to the bottom of the globe without him noticing. He is not that clever! I ran a DNA test and have created a DNA profile of him. This does not match any of our database records at the moment.

It is only a matter of time before he is caught!

Best wishes,

Dani Day
Senior Scientist, NICE

**Things to do**

**Write an email to Dani from Charles telling her what to do/try next.**

# WANTED!

## Collector Still at Large!

**Last seen:** Greenville hospital. He was posing as a patient with a broken arm.

**Description:** Dark hair. Brown eyes. 182 centimetres tall. Snappy dresser. Bionic hand. Spectrum retina enhanced implant.

**Crimes:** Theft of the entire population of cod in the North Atlantic. Theft of the White Cliffs of Dover. Attempted theft of the Sphinx at Giza. The robbery failed, but he did get away with the Sphinx's nose.

**Other info:** He likes to send snow globes to his victims.

Call Inspector Textor immediately on: Greenville 332 211

**Write a story about why the Collector might have been in the hospital. Write it from the point of view of the Collector, a doctor or of one of the other patients.**

# Broken bones and breakthroughs

Have you seen anyone with their arm or leg in plaster? You may even have had to wear a plaster yourself. Bones are tough, but they can snap if you have an accident. Broken or cracked bones are known as fractures. There are many different types of fracture.

**Some different types of fractures**

- Transverse fracture: a straight break across the bone
- Oblique fracture: the bone is broken at a slanted angle
- Spiral fracture: the bone is twisted and broken
- Longitudinal fracture: the bone is broken along its length
- Compression fracture: where the bone is crushed
- Open fracture: the bone breaks through the skin

**Repairing bones**

Bones can heal themselves. When your bone breaks the blood vessels inside will rupture (burst). Blood swells at the site of the fracture. This is eventually replaced by tissue called cartilage, then new bone.

However, it is important that bones heal in the right way … this is where the doctors come in. A doctor will need to find out which bone is broken and what kind of fracture it is. They will take an X-ray to find this out. Larger breaks may need pins to hold the ends of the bone securely together. Plates, wires, screws, rods and nails can also be used if the bone is broken in several places.

Broken bones need time to heal – usually about 6–8 weeks. To stop them moving and speed recovery, they are often surrounded with a plaster cast. These are made from bandages soaked in plaster. The plaster hardens to form a tough shell.

**Balloons could mend broken bones!**

Tiny micro-balloons, filled with 'bone cement', could soon be implanted into broken bones to help fractures to heal more quickly. It could do away with the need for metal plates, screws or rods to secure broken bones. Because surgeons don't need to slice through muscle or tissue to implant it, patients can recover much more quickly.

Scientists are always looking for new ways to help speed up medical procedures and reduce healing time and pain. Some of the biggest breakthroughs are the smallest in size ...

# Where science fiction and science meet ...

## Microbots to Save Lives!

**January 2009**

Tiny remote-controlled robots, small enough to swim up arteries (blood vessels that carry blood round the body), could soon save lives.

A team of researchers from Monash University in Australia, lead by Professor James Friend, are putting the finishing touches to the design. The aim is to produce microbot motors 250 micrometres ( $\frac{1}{4}$ of a millimetre) wide – so small that they can be injected into the human bloodstream.

The hope is that they will be able to reach parts of the body that have not been reached before. Information from the microbot could help to treat stroke victims, e.g. by helping to clear blockages in the bloodstream.

## Mini Submarines To Explore Human Body

**(January 2009)**

Plans for a nano-sized submarine, small enough to go inside the human body, have been developed. The next step for Dr Dan Peer and his team at Tel Aviv University in Israel, is for them to actually build the machine.

The submarine is designed to deliver drugs to specific cells in the body, in order to help cancer treatment and other disorders. They plan to launch their medical submarines, within three to five years.

Wow! I wonder what they will think of next?

BLEEP!

## Laser Space Probe To Help Prevent Blindness (January 2009)

A cataract is a problem with the lens in the eye. It becomes cloudy and blurred and can lead to blindness. Cataracts normally happen in older people, but if detected early enough, steps can be taken to help slow or stop the cataract developing. A new laser probe, originally developed for the space programme in the US, may be able to help detect the condition earlier than is otherwise possible.

**Imagine you are a journalist reporting on a new discovery. Write an article about it.**

# X-craft EXPLAINED

## The Green Dart

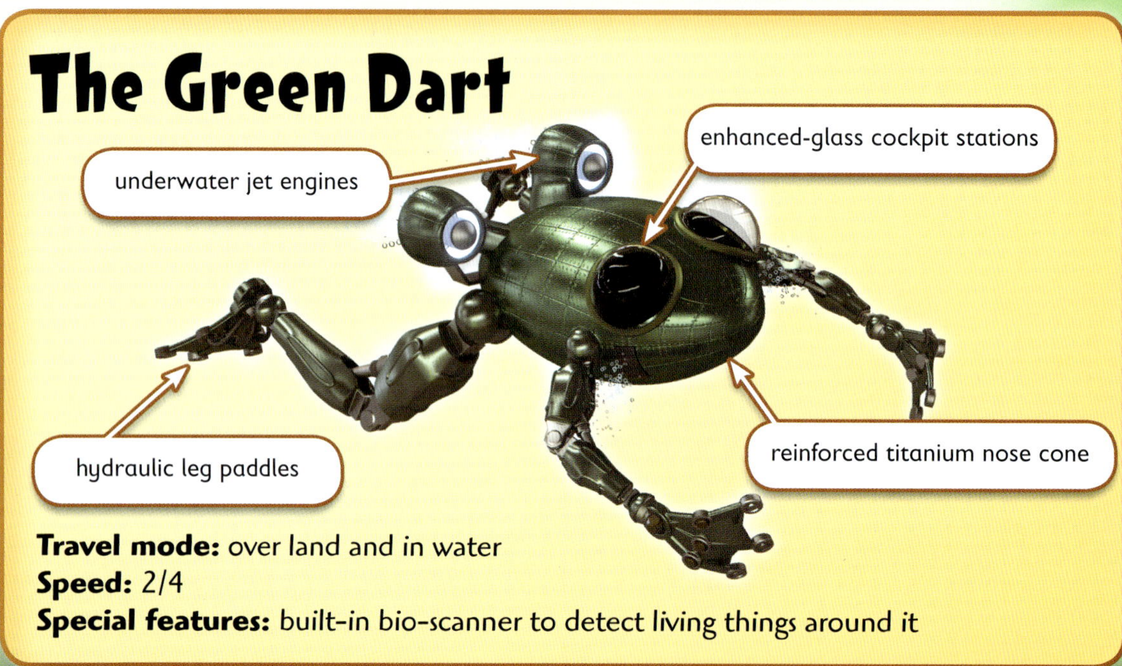


**Travel mode:** over land and in water
**Speed:** 2/4
**Special features:** built-in bio-scanner to detect living things around it

## The Grass Chopper

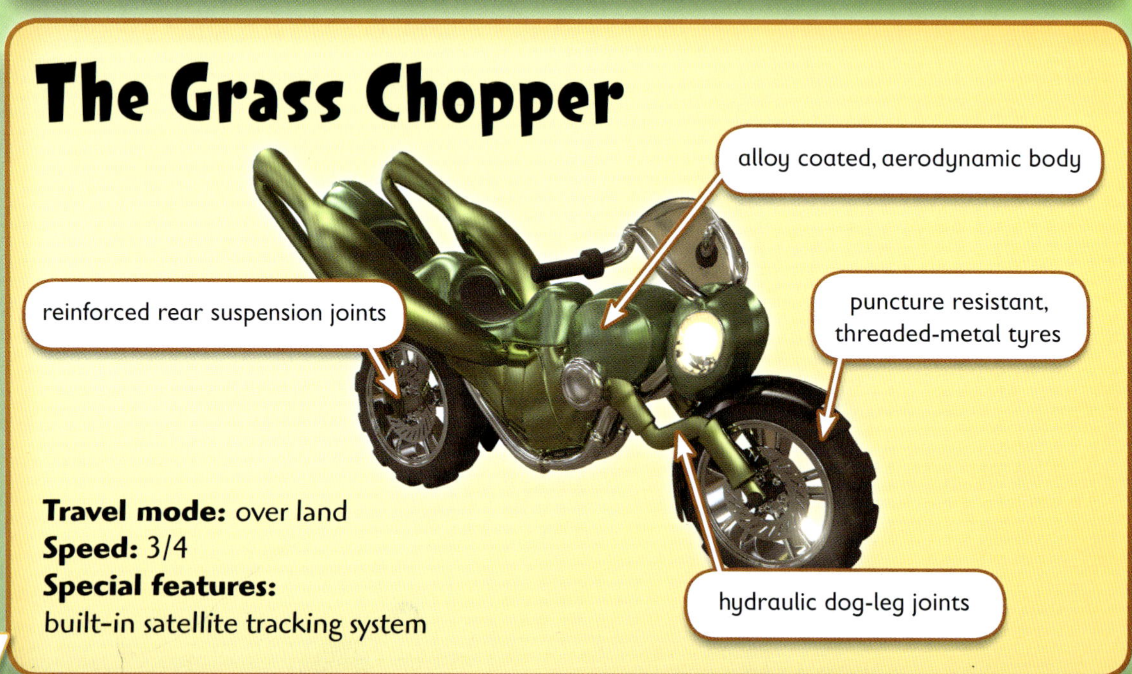


**Travel mode:** over land
**Speed:** 3/4
**Special features:**
built-in satellite tracking system

# Hawkwing

avian developed spoiler system
alloy coated, aerodynamic fuselage
turbo-boosted jet engines
hypersensitive ailerons

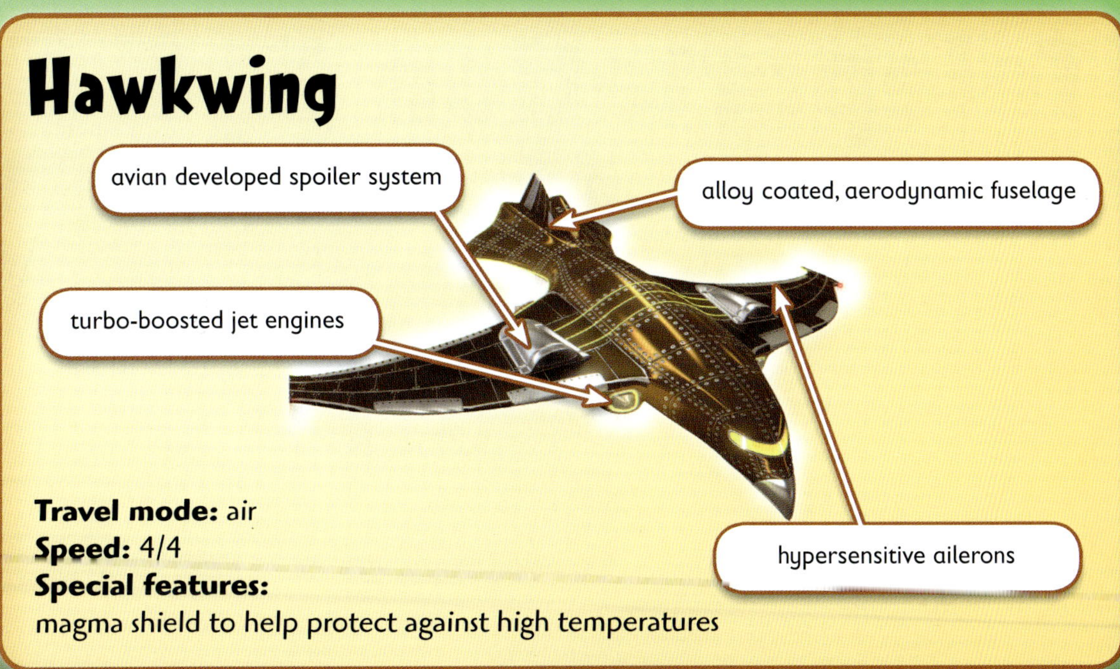

**Travel mode:** air
**Speed:** 4/4
**Special features:**
magma shield to help protect against high temperatures

# The Driller

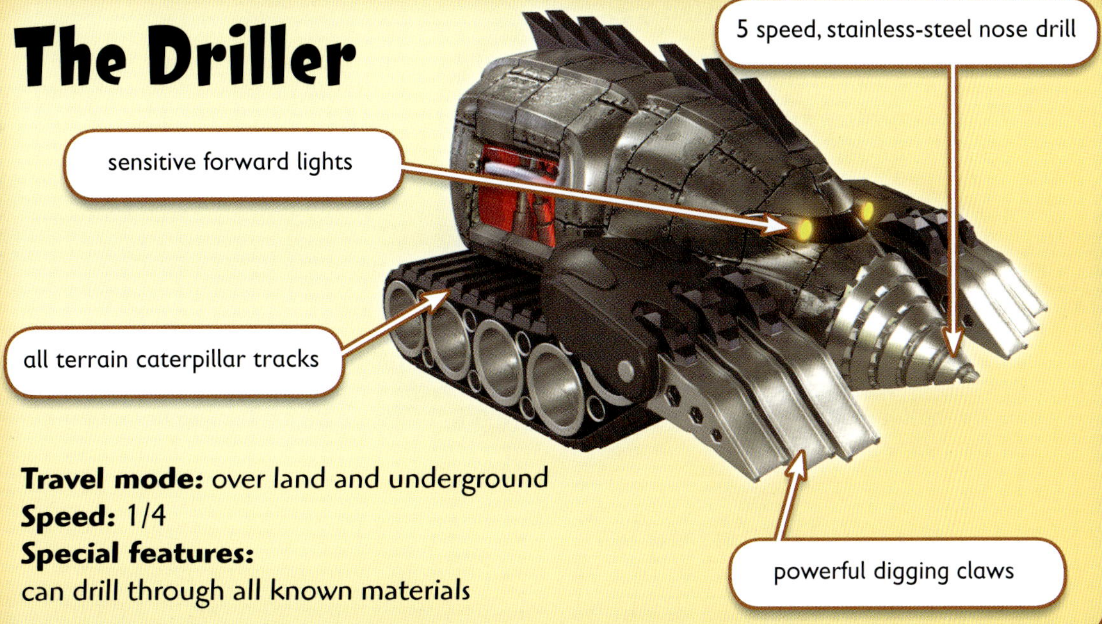

5 speed, stainless-steel nose drill
sensitive forward lights
all terrain caterpillar tracks
powerful digging claws

**Travel mode:** over land and underground
**Speed:** 1/4
**Special features:**
can drill through all known materials

**Things to do**

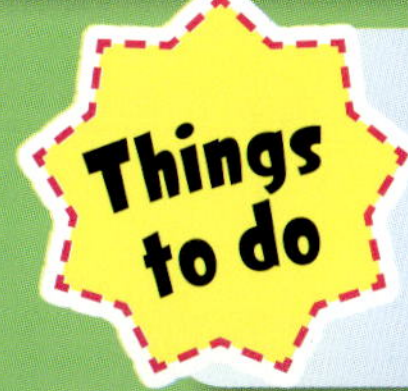

**Design your own new craft. What is it called? What special features does it have?**

# Teleportation

Can you imagine travelling to the other side of the world in a couple of seconds? There are lots of films and books where characters do this. They usually use some kind of teleport device. But could scientists actually build a machine like this?

The answer is that human teleportation is way beyond current technology, but it could be possible in the future.

A scientist conducts a teleportation experiment at the University of Innsbruck, Austria.

## The problem with humans ...

To teleport a human, one theory suggests that you would need to 'copy' them and then replicate (make another copy of) them in another place. The problem is that to do this you would need to know where every atom in that person's body was and how they link to each other. An atom is a tiny piece of matter found in each cell in your body – there are trillions and trillions of atoms inside you! There is no machine able to store this amount of data. Even if it were possible, what would you do with the original copy of the human – would it be deleted?

## Wormhole theory

Another idea about teleportation is that you could use a wormhole (see page 20). This would be like a door that you could walk through, so there would be no need to make copies of people. The problem is creating the wormhole in the first place ... we can't even be sure they exist at the moment.

### Some successful experiments

- 1998 – a group of physicists at the California Institute of Technology managed to teleport a photon. A photon is a particle of light. They teleported it about a metre. Once the replica appeared, the original disappeared.
- 2002 – researchers in Australia teleported a laser beam.
- 2006 – in Denmark a team of scientists teleported another laser beam. This one teleported two things – the light beam itself and the information stored in it. They sent it about half a metre.

# The X-gate

## Did you know ...

The word *teleport* comes from the Greek word *telos* (meaning 'far off' or 'distant') and the Latin word *portare* (meaning 'to carry'). *Teleportation* is the instant transfer of objects or matter from one place to another. The object doesn't actually move through space though, it disappears and then reappears.

X-portal: creates a wormhole effect.

Why not design your own teleport machine?

Containment field: stops everything in room being sucked in.

Silver box: magnifies residue energy left over from five micro-power supplies.

Computer panel: destination coordinates are typed in here.

**Things to do**

**Work with a partner. Imagine one of you is a scientist and the other is a reporter. The person playing the reporter can interview the scientist on how the X-gate works. The scientist has to make up an explanation.**

# The Collector's hideout

For more details on the Collector see pages 2–5 and page 8.

This may look like a normal picture frame, but really it's a secret screen where the Collector can watch his Master-bot at work.
This false fireplace is really an exit portal so that the Collector can make a quick getaway.
The Collector plans his evil schemes from this Dead Comfy 008 chair.
Things to do
Imagine you have entered this room for the first time. Talk with a partner about what you can see, smell and hear. What might be in the desk drawers? What's in the snow globes?

**Things to do**

This message was sent to Inspector Textor at the Greenville City Police Department by the Collector. Why do you think he sent it? Imagine you are the inspector. Make a list of all the things that you think the Collector could be planning.